WORKBOOK

Riding the Waves of Tribulation in Your Marriage, God's Way

Your Marriage Can Grow Stronger in the Midst of Turbulent Times!

Joe and Michelle Williams

Marriage911Godsway.com

Joe and Michelle Williams
Marriage911Godsway.com

©2000 *by Joe and Michelle Williams*
Revised, 2002, 2015, 2018

EABooks Publishing,
a division of Living Parables of Central Florida, Inc.
eabookspublishing.com

A special thank-you to those who shared their stories and continue to ride the waves—God's Way

Cover photo and all photos for all lessons with the exception of Two, Six, and Eight are by:

Matthew Cappuccilli Photography, OceanCappo.com— "Promoting God's Creation One Pic at a Time"

Back cover author photo by Chelsea Izzo

CONTENTS

INTRODUCTION

Have you ever wondered why some marriages fall apart during tough times and others make it through? Have you wondered how your marriage would fare if a wave of tribulation came crashing in on it? Or maybe you don't have to wonder—maybe you have already faced marital tribulations, and your marriage didn't fare well at all.

Because we have served in the ministry of troubled marriages since 1991, we have witnessed many couples separate or divorce in the midst of turbulent times. On the other hand, we have also been blessed by watching couples stand firm in their faith and ride out their wave with supernatural strength. Mark and Debbie were one of those couples. We met them in 1992 when their marriage was on the brink of divorce. After a lot of prayer, accountability and hard work, they reconciled, and one year later they began serving with us in the reconciliation ministry. When we founded our nonprofit, faith-based organization, The International Center for Reconciling God's Way, Inc. in 1999, we asked them to serve on our Board of Directors. *Riding the Waves of Tribulation in Your Marriage, God's Way* was first written in 2000 and Mark and Debbie co-led with us in teaching the principles in this book as well as our other reconciliation resources. They knew that couples in crisis could face anything as long as God was their anchor. What they didn't know however, was that their own tsunami was on its way.

On a sunny weekend, while spending time at their family cabin in Lake Tahoe, California, Mark and Debbie received a phone call that would turn their world, as they knew it, upside down. It was the phone call all parents dread. Their 23-year-old son had been killed in a tragic accident. Debbie recalls the heartache as if it were yesterday. "People kept asking, 'what do you need, what can I do for you?' All I could answer was, 'I want my son back! That's all I want!' I honestly thought that I would never be able to smile or laugh again."

Mark and Debbie's wave of tribulation in their marriage brought back old memories and they found themselves fighting to stay on top of the waves. Even though it was difficult, they refused to give in to old behaviors that would end in another separation. Together they made a commitment to dig deep and use the tools they had learned and taught over the years, and their marriage survived.

Today, when they teach reconciliation classes or speak on the loss of a child, they remind couples that it's not "if", but "when" the waves will come, and the time to prepare is now. "These tools are not a program. They are a lifestyle. Our marriage not only survived, but thrived in the midst of our storm because we put into practice what we knew worked. This workbook is a lifeline that you can use in the midst of your turbulent times, or prepare for the one that may be coming." Just as an experienced surfer faces huge waves with confidence, *Riding the Waves of Tribulation in Your Marriage, God's Way* will equip you to do the same.

The divorce rate among Christians is staggering, and one of the reasons is because couples don't ask for help until they're in the midst of a crisis. But by the time a couple is in a severe crisis, they oftentimes don't have the energy they need to save their sinking marriage. The best time to get help is when both spouses are still committed to making the marriage work, and preferably before a crisis. That is what this workbook, *Riding the Waves of Tribulation in Your Marriage--God's Way*, is designed to help you do.

HOW TO USE THE WORKBOOK

In this workbook, the Bible will often be referred to as your "suffer-board". The goal is to help you get into the habit of learning to go to God's Word when the suffering comes in your marriage, or any other area of your life. Our prayer for you is that when the waves of tribulation come, you will think of God's Word — the Bible — as your suffer-board and that you will stand on it as you ride your wave — God's way.

The principles shared and the lessons you will be asked to complete are based on biblical truths as well as the experience of others. Remember that God's Word and His truths will always produce peace and joy beyond human understanding for those who persevere — especially in times of suffering.

"...so is my word that goes out from my mouth: It will not return to me empty, but will accomplish what I desire and achieve the purpose for which I sent it. You will go out in joy and be led forth in peace..." (Isaiah 55: ll-12a).

This resource can be used as a couple, individually, or in a class or small group. The weekly discussion questions are designed to be reflective, or to discuss with a spouse, friend, or in a group setting. (Questions #1 and #2 on Introductory Week are for a group setting.) If you plan to facilitate a class or small group, please see Facilitator Guidelines at back of book.

BEFORE YOU BEGIN

Imagine that there were two brothers who loved to go surfing together every weekend. They lived for the big waves. When a storm came, they were excited because they knew that it would generate big waves. But one brother moved to the city and wasn't able to practice surfing for a whole year. Who do you think was the better surfer the following summer? The brother who had been able to practice, of course. So, grab your surfboard (or, "suffer-board" — the Bible) and get ready to learn to ride the waves of tribulation in your marriage — God's way!

INTRODUCTORY WEEK DISCUSSION QUESTIONS

Please be sensitive and respectful toward your spouse when sharing anything about your marriage relationship in a group setting.

1. How many years have you been married, and how many children do you have?

2. Are you a blended family?

3. What is at least one quality that you admire in your spouse?

4. Recall an event or time (such as a vacation or a special date) that you and your spouse still refer to as one of your best memories together.

5. Do you and your spouse presently attend a church, Bible study, or a Christian support group of any kind?

6. If so, what is it?

LESSON ONE

SURF'S UP!

Tribulations and Turbulent Time in Marriage Often Produce the Biggest Waves in Life.

"It is better, if it is God's will, to suffer for doing good than for doing evil" (1 Peter 3:17).

Do you realize that the waves you see on a sunny day at the beach are actually a result of wind from a storm that you *can't* see? The same is true when waves crash in on the shore of your marriage. You may be experiencing a "sunny day" when, all of a sudden, the waves from a storm that has been brewing catch you off guard. With practice, you can learn to ride the waves of tribulation in your marriage with the same joy that a surfer rides the storm-produced waves on the ocean.

"The surf that distresses the ordinary swimmer produces in the surf-rider the super-joy of going clean through it. Apply that to our own circumstances, these very things — tribulation, distress, persecution, (to) produce in us the super-joy; they are not things to fight. We are more than conquerors through Him in all these things, not in spite of them, but in the midst of them. The saint never knows the joy of the Lord in spite of tribulation, but because of it…" Oswald Chambers, <u>My Utmost for His Highest,</u> March 7.

From Joe and Michelle:

"It took us several years to learn how to ride the waves in our marriage. We really didn't understand that the waves that hit us could actually be an opportunity to grow us closer to God and to strengthen our marriage. Because we serve in a ministry to help save marriages — which Satan hates — we know that we are targets for his attacks. We also know that if we don't prepare for those attacks by being in God's Word constantly, praying together, and staying accountable to a group of Christians, we won't be able to stand up under the trials and tribulations that will come our way. There have been many times that we have failed when a wave crashed in on us, but we have learned how to quickly get back on our 'suffer-board' (the Bible) and catch the next wave that comes."

Most of the couples that have reconciled their marriage share that they stopped using the words "divorce" or "separation" in their vocabulary, and made a solid commitment to their marriage. Yet many confess that they still struggle with behavior that is less than godly in the midst of stressful circumstances.

For You to Consider:

Choose one or more of the following behaviors that you would be willing to work on over the next few weeks when trials and tribulations come your way.

☐ Attitude

☐ Self-control (anger issues)

☐ Verbal abuse

☐ Withdrawing

☐ Other:

Action:

Look up Romans 5:3-4 and James 1:2-4, and answer the following questions.

1. What do these verses have in common?

2. According to these verses, what should you do when you are faced with problems?

Many couples struggle in the area of forgiveness. Marriages end simply because one partner blames the other for the "storm" in their marriage. But, forgiveness is just the beginning of the reconciliation and restoration process after a wave hits a marriage. If you want to make sure that your marriage can survive a crisis, you must understand the importance of forgiveness and practice it on a daily basis.

Forgiveness is giving up your right to retaliate—even if your spouse doesn't repent or stop behavior that is ungodly. You must allow God to work in you and not harbor bitterness. Forgiveness is the first step to reconciliation.

Forgiveness does not mean that the person you are forgiving did not do something wrong or hurtful.

Reconciliation requires a heart attitude of forgiveness and repentance from both of you, and a willingness to let go of the issues that caused the disagreement (or separation). Reconciliation after a disagreement or major problem in your marriage is difficult, but the rewards are huge.

Restoration is the repairing of the marriage after a serious storm, and it takes place over a period of time—sometimes even years. It requires daily focus on giving up selfish desires for the lifetime of the marriage. The restoration process takes time and much practice with the "suffer-board" (Bible). If you have ever been separated or considered divorce you have probably had to experience this aspect in the reconciliation process.

For You to Consider:

Can you truthfully say that you do not harbor any bitterness against your spouse? How about any other important relationship? Is there anyone else in your life (parents, children, etc.) with whom you feel God wants you to reconcile? A relationship that is not reconciled and restored because of your refusal to forgive can actually affect your marriage relationship. But more importantly it affects your relationship with God.

Action:

1. Take time this week to pray about all of your relationships and ask God to reveal anyone that you need to forgive. Once you have forgiven the person in your heart, God will show you the next step. Trust Him and focus on Him as you move towards being at peace with others (see Matthew, 5: 8-10).

2. If you have recently reconciled with your spouse or come through a severe tribulation in your marriage, are you willing to spend whatever time it takes to restore your relationship? Stop now and pray for God's supernatural strength to get you through this. If you have never trusted Jesus as Savior and Lord of your life, ask Him now. If you are a Christian but you have walked away from God, take the time to recommit your life to Him.

It's natural to suffer in marriage because it is hard work to restore the relationship after a crisis. So you will need the Supernatural. There are plenty of married couples that boast of their years together, but behind closed doors their hearts have hardened towards one another, and they suffer in silence as a result of not spending the time necessary to restore their relationship—God's way. All marriages will experience tribulation waves, especially when trying to live for Christ. But, by choosing to allow God to work His will in whatever tribulation might occur, He will lift you on top of the waves!

"…the peace of God which surpasses all understanding will guard your hearts and minds through Christ Jesus our Lord" (Philippians 4:7).

"Yes, and all who desire to live godly lives in Christ Jesus will suffer persecution" (2 Timothy 3:12).

> Spouses who do not forgive experience marriage as a three-ring ceremony:
>
> HIS RING, HER RING, and the "SUFFER-RING"

We will all suffer for one reason or another, but as a believer you shouldn't suffer because of making choices outside of God's will for your life. The suffering experienced as a follower of Christ is the kind of suffering that produces growth and maturity.

Action:

1. Look up Philippians 1:29. What has been granted to you as a believer?

2. What does Jesus say about suffering in John 16:33? What should your attitude be?

Don't miss an important truth found in God's Word concerning suffering. Suffering is necessary in order to mature. Many marriages end in separation and divorce because of the desire to have peace and happiness without suffering. Over the following weeks you will begin to view the tribulations in your marriage as opportunities to grow together and to mature in your Christian walk. Rather than feeling hopeless and frustrated, you can feel hopeful and motivated. Since suffering is part of life and granted to us by God, we are told in 1 Peter 3:17 that we should suffer for doing good rather than because of any evil on our part. How we choose to respond to tribulations can cause painful consequences in our life and in the lives of our loved ones.

For You to Consider:

How many times have you suffered because of a choice your spouse made? And, more importantly, how many times has your spouse suffered because of your choices?

There is no other relationship between two people on earth more important than that of a husband and wife (Ephesians 5:31-33), and oftentimes there is no other relationship more difficult.

Action:

1. The next time you suffer because of something you have said or done, do what's necessary to repent and make things right. Then pray for God's wisdom and strength to endure the consequence as if you were a surfer riding a wave — a little fearful, but practicing with God at your side. When the wave of tribulation is over, look for ways to ride it better next time. Identify how your faith in God is stronger because of riding it with Him rather than alone.

2. The next time you suffer because of someone else's choice, pray that God will give you the wisdom and strength to lift that person in prayer and avoid retaliation or bitterness.

Regardless of the reason you suffer, God is always in control and you will always have something to learn from the experience.

Please answer Discussion Questions on the next page.

LESSON ONE DISCUSSION QUESTIONS

Please remember to be sensitive and respectful toward your spouse when sharing anything about your marriage relationship in a group setting.

1. Share your thoughts on the idea of suffering based on the Scriptures that were provided in this week's lesson.

2. Discuss the definitions of forgiveness, reconciliation, and restoration as explained in Lesson One. If possible, share a personal experience of a time you had to first forgive before you could reconcile.

3. Discuss any of the verses that especially spoke to you in this lesson.

4. Did you have an opportunity this week to implement any of the actions? Share at least one action with your group.

5. Review your answers and prepare to discuss.

Close in Prayer

LESSON TWO

HOT-DOGGIN'

Jesus was the only one who ever walked on water without sinking.
Do you really think you can ride the waves of tribulation in life in your own strength?

"Pride goes before destruction, a haughty spirit before a fall"
(Proverbs 16:18).

When an experienced surfer has the opportunity to ride the perfect wave on a perfect day with others watching, his ability to perform stunts and maneuvers might cause him or her to show off—"hot-doggin" as they used to say back in the day—in a way that ends up being anything but humble.

To believe that God will give us everything we want from our spouse and marriage and protect us from troubles just because we've asked and practiced with our suffer-board is prideful and self-centered. God will always continue to grow us through troubles, and He wants us to trust Him in the midst.

"The first thing God does is to knock pretense and the pious pose right out of me. ...God loved me not because I was lovable, but because it was His nature to do so. ...He says to me, 'show the same love to others—Love as I have loved you. I will bring any number of people about you whom you cannot respect, and you must exhibit My love to them as I have exhibited it to you.'" —Oswald Chambers, My Utmost for His Highest, May 11.

Consider what God might think of the following prayer:

"Dear Lord, I come to you this morning with much humility. You know how godly I am. I study your word daily, and my weekly Bible study questions are completed on time before anyone else's in my group. I'm never late for church, and you know how I never miss serving in little Johnny's Sunday school class. I know that if I ask anything in Your name You will give it to me. So, I'm asking you this: Could you please take all my troubles away and could you please change my spouse so that I can have a happy marriage?"

Obviously, this prayer is not one of humility, but of pride and self-centeredness. But how often do some of the requests we make to the Lord sound just as bad, because deep in the recesses of our hearts we believe we deserve to be happy—especially if we are doing our part?

Action:

1. Look up Matthew 7:1-5, and write what it says to you personally.

2. Jesus is clear about getting the plank out of our own eye before helping others get the speck out of theirs. But it takes prayer and discipline to be able to identify our own self-centeredness and avoid hot-doggin', especially in marriage. Typically, when there is a problem, we want to point the finger at the other person and put blame on anyone but ourselves. But, in reality, if we would just follow the example of what Jesus said in the above Scripture verses, it would make the problem much easier to handle. We have no control over how other people behave, but we must learn to take full responsibility for our own actions. This will make the situation at hand less complicated. A self-centered response makes a bad situation worse.

3. Look up the following words in a Dictionary, and write the main point in each definition.

    • Pride:

    • Humility:

    • Meek:

Regardless of your summary for each word, you no doubt saw Christ's character defined in the last two words and the quality that God hates the most in the first word.

For You to Consider:

Why do you think pride is something that the Lord wants us to avoid as a character quality?

Action:

1. Look up Philippians 4:5-6. Personalize the verses by inserting your name throughout the verses.

2. What do the verses say you should do when faced with tribulation? Why do you think it is so difficult?

3. Why do you think presenting your requests to God can help in the area of pride?

4. Why do you think it's important to present your requests with an attitude of thanksgiving?

Christ says we must have humility in order to be thankful (humble) in all circumstances. When we are prideful, our trust is on man's ability rather than God's.

Action:

"Do nothing out of selfish ambition or vain conceit, but in humility consider others before yourself. Each of you should look not only to your own interests, but also to the interests of others. Your attitude should be that of Christ Jesus" (Philippians 2: 3-5).

1. Does the above verse say that you should only look out for others and not for your own interests? What do you think is the main point of the verse, and how do you think you can have a better attitude towards your spouse when a crisis hits your marriage.

2. Do you feel exhausted at times? It's natural and normal for exhaustion to occur when you have a family to care for, along with the daily demands in life. Jesus took time to rest, pray alone, and to get replenished. And He was God. Don't make the mistake of thinking that you are stronger than God when it comes to taking time out to be replenished. Admit that you are tired or overworked and talk to your spouse about how you might rearrange your schedule to add time for yourself, or balance your schedule to include more time for family fun. If you are worn out trying to meet the needs of your spouse and children, along with the demands of a job, ministry, or other outside obligations, you will need to make sure that you nurture yourself in order to avoid becoming resentful and burnt out. Once resentment begins, it is impossible to have a Christ-like attitude in anything.

3. Are you facing a problem which has nothing to do with your spouse, but has to do with an outside attack? Some examples are,

    *   Legal
    *   Extended family
    *   Children
    *   Illness
    *   Financial
    *   Death of a loved one

- Caring for elderly
- Other

Action

1. Read Romans: 12:9-21. What is Paul's main point? You can choose to see your circumstance as an opportunity to trust God and mature in your Christian walk as you learn to persevere, which ultimately produces Christ-like character and hope.

2. Look up Romans 5:3-4 once more, and share your thoughts in light of this concept.

From Michelle:

"When my husband, Joe, and I first reconciled after being separated for two years, I moved into his small brown duplex. Our son and I had been staying with my mom for a while to save money. After a few days, I asked Joe when we were going to move into a nicer home together. His reply made me think that I had made the wrong decision to reconcile. He explained that he wanted us to learn to be happy where we were. He believed that if I needed a certain house to be happy — or anything else outside of my relationship with the Lord and each other, for that matter — that our marriage relationship would never be solid. He knew that I would never be satisfied. I didn't realize it for a few months, but he was absolutely right. We had lived above our means prior to our separation and we had gotten into a bad habit of looking for satisfaction in material things rather than in our relationship with God and with each other. So when I moved into his brown duplex (everything was brown: the carpet, the wall trim, the outside; and there was one window — it was bleak, to say the least), he knew it would stretch us, but that we would learn to be grateful wherever God placed us. This was difficult, since I expected that my willingness to reconcile and work on the marriage would be rewarded with many blessings from God — including a beautiful home.

In the months that followed (and after a few fits), I finally resigned myself to living in the duplex indefinitely. I have to admit that I learned to be content as I got creative and changed my thinking. I pretended that we lived in a hotel (after all, they're small and sometimes brown) and I decorated it with white wicker furniture and sea-foam green pillows, painted the trim white and hung pictures of ocean scenes everywhere. I actually liked it. So when my husband suggested that we move into a nice home in a great part of town, I wasn't even sure I wanted to go! We did move, but to this day we refer to any tribulation that challenges us in the area of contentment as a "brown duplex opportunity."

For You to Consider:

Have you and your spouse had to learn to be content in difficult circumstances? Are you presently learning contentment? If so, in which area of your life?

Action:

1. Once a week for the remainder of the class, help someone less fortunate than you. If your spouse is willing to participate, it would be a great opportunity to serve together. You could choose to spend time with an elderly person, help at a homeless shelter, or even ask God to show you someone each week that you could give a helping hand.

2. Sometime over the next few weeks, take the opportunity to ask your spouse if there is any area in your life that is out of balance or needs attention (be sure to be prayed up before you do this). Ask God to give you a quiet and gentle spirit as you listen to what he or she says, and be willing to give whatever suggestions are offered a try.

3. Get into the habit of saying "thank you" to God every time you are faced with a problem or trial of any kind. This habit will help you focus on Him and His promises as you grow through the experience, and help you learn contentment in whatever circumstance you are facing.

    Example: "Lord, I don't like this and I feel scared, but thank you anyway. I will trust you to walk with me every step of the way." Thanking God for even the smallest troubles will help you get into the habit of riding the waves of tribulation in your marriage and life with a grateful heart.

4. If you enjoy writing, consider keeping a praise journal. On a regular basis, list all the things you are grateful for in your life. There's a lot to be said about counting your blessings, and it will be a great reminder of all that God has provided — even in stressful times.

Pride versus humility: Pride leads to disgrace, quarrels,
punishment and destruction.
Humility leads to wisdom, accepting advice,
and honor.

See Proverbs: 11:2; 13:10; 15:33, 16:5, 18, and 29:23.

Please answer Discussion Questions on the next page.

LESSON TWO DISCUSSION QUESTIONS

Please remember to be sensitive and respectful toward your spouse when sharing anything about your marriage relationship.

1. Discuss your response to Matthew 7:1-5.

2. Share your dictionary answers on Action question #2.

3. Discuss at least one of your answers to Action questions #1-4.

4. Have you had an opportunity this week to say "thank you to God" when you were faced with a problem? Have you and your spouse been able to do this together?

Close in Prayer

LESSON THREE

UNDERCURRENT

What undercurrents are waiting to take you down?

"Therefore each of you must put off falsehood and speak truthfully to his neighbor, for we are all members of one body. In your anger do not sin... Do not give the devil a foothold" (Ephesians 4:25-27).

Surfers know it's not just the big waves that can cause serious problems for a swimmer. The swift water beneath the surface of the waves along the beach (or undercurrent) can pull a swimmer down when they least expect it. If you and your spouse reconcile after a separation or you successfully ride a wave of tribulation from something outside your marriage, you will need to guard against the temptation to sit back and "bask in the sunshine." It will be important to continue practicing with your suffer-board. Many marriages end simply because of years spent never dealing with the little, unnoticeable things in marriage and taking each other for granted.

"You have remained true to God under great and intense trials; now beware of the undercurrent. Do not be morbidly introspective, looking forward with dread, but keep alert; keep your memory bright before God. Kept by the power of God- that is the only safety." — Oswald Chambers, My Utmost for His Highest, April 19.

One example of an undercurrent that can exist between couples is the fear of a spouse's reaction to unpleasant situations. If either spouse fears speaking up or tells little white lies in order to avoid conflict, there is an undercurrent in their marriage. Many of the couples learn to suppress their real feelings in order to keep peace or to manipulate circumstances and it's just a matter of time until the marriage is in crisis.

Don't fall to pieces trying to keep the peace.

From Darrel:

"I just don't like confrontation, so I would rather not discuss issues or tell my wife something if I think she will get upset. For instance, right now money is tight, but I just pay whatever bills I can and let the rest go, instead of telling the kids they can't have something or not allow them to go to camp. I don't want to let my family know how bad our financial situation really is."

Darrel's situation did finally blow up when his wife intercepted a call from one of their creditors. They both realized that how they expressed anger and honesty toward each other were two of the weakest areas in their marriage. It took classes, counseling, and a lot of practice before they learned that taking the risk to be real with each other was the catalyst that brought them closer and saved their marriage.

While suppressed anger and honesty can be very dangerous in marriage, there is another behavior just as serious, and that is secret sin. Many people deal with stress in their life by deadening the emotions and replacing their pain with a secret sin. Happiness is their focus and feeling good is their ultimate goal. But the end result is having an undercurrent in their marriage.

Secret sins include:

- Alcohol or drug addiction (either illegal or prescription)
- Sexual or adulterous relationships—whether it be physical, emotional, online or through social media or texting
- Secret charge cards or loans
- Gambling
- Pornography
- Lewd or illegal behavior

These secret sins do not necessarily need to be a secret from your spouse. In fact, in some cases, the spouse may even join in—possibly to avoid the consequences of not participating.

Karen's story:

When Karen called the ministry for help, she wanted advice regarding a situation in her marriage. Over a twelve-year period she had spent all of the family's savings trying to manage their farm, and her husband didn't know. Rather than inform him that there wasn't enough money each month, she chose to protect him. But instead, she created an undercurrent in their marriage. Our prayer team prayed with her and encouraged her to fear God more than her husband and to take the risk to be real with him—regardless of the consequences—and bring everything into the light. She admitted that while spending the money was the main area of deception, she had been deceitful in other areas as well. We encouraged her to make a list of every hidden thing that the Lord brought to her mind and to confess it all at once rather than a little at a time. We have continued to keep in touch over the years, and she has given us permission to print her story. Her husband forgave her and admitted that he actually felt relief when his wife confessed, because he had suspected for quite some time that she was being deceitful. There were consequences, of course, but the Lord blessed her obedience more than she could have imagined. A couple of years later, Karen began heading up a community prayer group in their town.

The wave of tribulation that Karen and her husband survived prepared them for a tsunami in their marriage five years later. Their 17-year-old daughter was tragically killed in an auto accident on Father's Day. Because they had come through their previous troubles by focusing on God and doing things right, they survived what many married couples cannot: the death of a child. Karen and her husband held on to each other and to God's promises. Karen recalled all the ways God had prepared them prior to their daughter's death, and she praised Him in the midst of such sadness. Losing a child is tough on a marriage. Riding out a wave such as this takes supernatural strength, but because they had been practicing with their "Suffer-Board", their marriage is still standing today.

For You to Consider:

Deceit creates an undercurrent in marriage, and it will result in letting the sun go down on your anger, and the devil will get a foothold—as Paul warns in Ephesians 4:25-27.

Action:

1. When you are tempted to be dishonest for any reason at all—regardless of how minor you think it is—ask yourself why you are fearful of being honest.

2. Stop at once and ask the Lord to help you choose truth rather than deceit.

3. Ask the Lord to show you anything that you have kept hidden from your spouse that he or she needs to know. This is a serious matter.

4. The Lord will equip you as you pray, so don't ignore this assignment. If you want to have a truly great marriage and learn to ride the waves of tribulation as they come, you must get rid of anything that will create an undercurrent that will ultimately give the devil a foothold in your marriage.

5. Once a week at least take stock before God and see whether you are keeping your life up to the standard He wishes.

"Paul is like a musician who does not heed the approval of the audience if he can catch the look of approval from his Master." — Oswald Chambers. <u>My Utmost for His Highest</u>, March 17

> Secret sin is detrimental to a marriage relationship and must
> be stopped at once if you want God to bless your marriage.

Action:

Look up 1 Peter 1:13-16 and answer the following questions.

1. What are you supposed to prepare your mind for, and how?

2. What do the words "self-control" and "alert" mean to you? What are some reasons that you can think of as to why someone would not have self-control or be alert?

3. Read 1 Peter 5: 6-10 and answer the following questions.

4. How much of your anxiety should you cast on God and how much should you keep for yourself?

5. Why should you be self-controlled and alert?

6. When does God restore us and make us strong?

Please answer Discussion Questions on the next page.

LESSON THREE DISCUSSION QUESTIONS

Please remember to be sensitive and respectful toward your spouse when sharing anything about your marriage relationship.

1. Discuss your answers to the verses in 1 Peter.

2. Were you raised thinking that it was okay to be dishonest in certain situations, and that little white lies were acceptable if it meant staying out of trouble with others? (This is not concerning life or death situations.) If so, discuss what you think about that now?

3. Do you have an example in your own marriage when you brought something into the light and your relationship grew closer as a result?

4. Choose a couple of the actions or verses that you would like to share in your group, along with Ephesians 4: 25-27.

Close in Prayer

LESSON FOUR

SURFER, BEWARE!

Beware, there's an enemy in the waters who wants to destroy your marriage and your relationship with God. Be prepared and alert, and remember—the enemy is not your spouse!

"Your enemy the devil prowls around like a roaring lion looking
for someone to devour" (1 Peter 5:8).

Good surfers know the importance of being self-controlled and alert. They must be aware at all times in order to avoid dangerous situations and circumstances. Sharks—referred to in surfing terms as the devil—want to attack and devour swimmers just as Satan wants to attack and devour marriages and destroy families. But, God has a plan for our lives and, in the midst of our trials, He wants us to draw near to Him and trust in Him. And, Satan has a plan too. When we face tribulation in this world, he wants us to do anything but draw near to God. We must be self-controlled and alert or we won't be able to pray and make wise decisions based on the Bible—our suffer-board.

"There are times when God will not lift the darkness from you, but trust Him. God will appear like an unkind friend, but He is not; He will appear like an unnatural Father, but He is not; He will appear like an unjust judge, but He is not. Keep the notion of the mind of God behind all things strong and growing. Nothing happens in any particular unless God's will is behind it, therefore you can rest in perfect confidence in Him. Prayer is not only asking, but an attitude of mind which produces the atmosphere in which asking is perfectly natural." — Oswald Chambers, My Utmost for His Highest, July 16.

For You to Consider:

When a wave of tribulation comes and you are suffering (because of your own sin, someone else's sin, or an unavoidable disaster), it's your perception of the situation that will determine how you will ride the wave. But your perception (which is the ability to attain understanding and awareness in an experience) is based on what you believe—or choose to believe—in the situation. How you choose to respond to the waves of tribulation in your life and your marriage relationship will depend on your view of God and how well you know and understand His Word.

Juan and Anita's Story:

After Juan was involved in an accident that caused the death of their small child, Anita shared their story and gave us permission to use it.

"When I got the phone call and realized our child was gone, I knew she was with the Lord and He was taking care of her. I also knew that my husband would blame himself for her death and that he needed me now more than ever. I had been studying about God's faithfulness in a Bible study and I was able— through the supernatural power of God—to forgive him and show him my love. All I could think of was that I'd lost my only child—I didn't want to lose my husband too."

Anita had a choice, and she chose to trust God. Satan worked hard on that couple, but they are together today and not only have two more children, but serve in ministry together in their church. Their marriage would never have survived if she had chosen to believe the lies that Satan tried to feed her. Yes, there was grief, and her husband has had some difficult times not blaming himself; but her choice to forgive him and stand on the truths of the suffer-board and view the tribulations in their marriage through God's eyes rather than the world's saved their marriage.

Action:

1. Choose to live by God's Truth and work from that premise. Remember that when God answers our prayers, it may not come in the way imagined. Learn to have God's perspective rather than man's.

2. In the opening verse of this lesson and in 1 Peter 5:8, and 1:13-16, Peter tells us to be self-controlled and alert. List some ways that you plan to do that.

3. List some of the ways that people tend to busy themselves rather than spend time practicing on their suffer-board when tribulations come into marriage.

4. Look up James 4:7. What is your responsibility, and what are you promised?

5. What commands are given in 1 Peter 4:7-10? According to verse 7, why are they so important?

"Satan doesn't have to get us thinking blatantly satanic thoughts to have victory over us. All he needs is to get us looking at life from man's perspective rather than God's. If we surrender our minds to the things of God, we are safe!" — Beth Moore, Jesus, the One and Only.

Peter commands us to be sober-minded, to think and act soberly, discreetly, to use sound judgment and moderation, to be self-disciplined because the end times are near. He is referring to the importance of keeping mentally alert and having self-control so that we are able to pray for and serve one another in the church.

For You to Consider:

How should you be living your life? Is there sin in your life that you have not confessed? If so, confess it now and pray for God's strength. Review the list of secret sins in last week's lesson. Ask the Lord to show you any area of your life where you are allowing things of the world or sinful choices to cloud your ability to think clearly or practice self-control. Confess this to your spouse and hold one another accountable in whatever area each of you might be struggling. If one of you suffers with an addiction of some kind, get into a Bible-based, Christian recovery or support group and place yourself under the authority of spiritually mature people who can pray for and with you regularly.

Action:

1. Ask God to show you ways that you can show your spouse love and support and yet not condone addiction or sin in your marriage.

2.   If possible, review this lesson with your spouse. If you are currently in crisis and your spouse is unwilling, choose a family member or close friend to do this with you. If you are struggling in any area at all that is causing you to lack self-control and not be alert, you will need the support from a loved one in order to have accountability.

3.   Get into the habit of noticing when your thoughts are going in a direction that ends up making you feel hopeless. That is always Satan's plan for you when you are facing tribulation in your marriage. God's plan is always one of hope!

SATAN'S PLAN

Doubt = Makes you question God's Word and His goodness.

Discouragement = Makes you look at your problems rather than God.

Diversion = Makes the wrong things seem attractive so that you will want them more than the right things.

Defeat = Makes you feel like a failure so that you don't even try.

Delay = Makes you put off doing something so that it never gets done.

All which ultimately leads to

Hopelessness = Believing that God is NOT in control and He's not there.

Chart taken from Life Application Bible (NIV)
Tyndale House Publishers, Inc., Wheaton, Illinois, and Zondervan Publishing House, Grand Rapids, Michigan. Page 13.

Please answer Discussion Questions on the next page.

LESSON FOUR DISCUSSION QUESTIONS

Please remember to be sensitive and respectful toward your spouse when sharing anything about your marriage relationship.

1. If you have asked Christ to be your Savior all your sins were forgiven—past, present, and future—at the time you accepted Him. However, your confession keeps you in right fellowship and in agreement with God (1 John 1:9). How do you think this principle helps couples have a stronger marriage?

2. Was there ever a time that God seemed like an unkind friend to you? Were you able to understand later that He was by your side—and even grieving with you when you were hurting?

3. Do you have a special Bible verse, or technique that helps you when Satan brings negative thoughts to your mind?

4. Review the lesson for this week and be prepared to share a few of the verses or actions. What did the Lord show you concerning the choices you should make when you face troubles in your life?

Close in Prayer

LESSON FIVE

WIPE OUT!

Yes, there will be tribulation waves in your life and marriage,
but you will only wipe out if you let go of your suffer-board!

"Therefore everyone who hears these words of mine and puts them into practice is like a wise man who built his house on the rock. The rain came down, the streams rose, and the winds blew and beat against that house; yet it did not fall, because it had its foundation on the rock. But everyone who hears these words of mine and does not put them into practice is like a foolish man who built his house on sand" (Matthew 7: 24-27).

If a surfer doesn't learn to use his or her board correctly, there will be more time spent in the water than on the board. Likewise, if your marriage isn't built correctly with unconditional love, commitment, and a spiritual foundation, the waves of tribulation all couples face will wipe you out. The term "wipe out" in this lesson refers to falling off your suffer-board or turning away from God and His promises. We see many couples grow apart and build walls of silence in their homes because of not turning to God and trusting Him with the disappointments of life. God cries with us. He cares. But if you don't let Him comfort you in the sad times you will put too much expectation on your spouse and you will be let down. So many couples expect their spouse to take away heartache and pain in a crisis, and most of the time their spouse is hurting as much as they are. God has numerous ways to comfort us during our tribulations. While He often uses our spouse, He also uses His Word, others, and the Holy Spirit in us.

"Sadly, most couples build their marriage the world's way; and rather than spending time with God daily, the only time they cry out to Him is when they're in trouble. If you go to Him to be guided, He will guide you; but He will not comfort your distrust or half-trust of Him by showing you the chart of all His purposes concerning you. He will show you only into a way where, if you go cheerfully and trustfully forward, He will show you on still farther." — Mrs. Charles E. Cowman, Streams in the Desert.

Fear and doubt during times of tribulation will take its toll on the marriage relationship. When we are stressed, we say and do things that we wouldn't do otherwise, and those we love are the ones who receive the brunt of our actions. If we learn to stand on the promises of God during a crisis, we won't destroy our loved ones—even when we're overwhelmed. To trust and obey God is to love Him, and our obedience—especially in times of trouble—is sweet to Him. He will always give us a way out after we have suffered a while. (See 1 Peter 5:10.)

For You to Consider:

Think of a time that you cried out to God for help, and when He sent it, you didn't recognize it until later.

Action:

1. Get into the habit of realizing that in the midst of every tribulation God is right there beside you. He hasn't forgotten you. If you turn your back on Him during your troubles, you will not be able to receive His peace and joy and supernatural strength in order to ride the wave—and that is when you will wipe out.

2. Read Matthew 26:36-41. Why was Jesus so adamant that the disciples should pray?

3. Read John 13:37-38. What did Peter think he would never do?

4. Read Luke 22:60-62. What did Peter do?

Peter walked with Jesus and yet he wiped out for a time. He felt hopeless, but Jesus restored him when he truly repented.

Marla's Story:

Tom and Marla's grown son and daughter-in-law drank too much and didn't control their tempers. In a heated argument one night, their son left his wife and children. Tom was frustrated with his son's behavior and wanted him to suffer the consequences of his refusal to live for Christ, while Marla believed that if they let their son move back home they could have a positive influence over him. She believed that their example of a good marriage and encouragement to attend an addiction recovery program at their church would result in repentance and a saved marriage. Things didn't work out as they had hoped.

"I should have listened to Tom, but I really believed we could save our son from more heartache and going off a cliff of despair if we were there for him. I couldn't have been more wrong. When our son moved home he wouldn't listen to our advice, and he refused to have anything to do with God and church. Instead he blamed God for his problems. To make matters worse, Tom and I started arguing, so my desire to have our son witness a Christ-like marriage became a challenge I didn't expect. Our son's problems had become ours. Our son didn't have consequences and was not suffering, so he had no reason to change."

Tom and Marla's situation is not uncommon. This ministry receives calls and emails regularly from parents who have grown children who are causing waves of tribulation in the family as a result of bad choices and not following God. If these desperate parents aren't standing on their suffer-board and living their own lives God's way, they can result in wiping out. Thankfully, in Tom and Marla's case, they were able to re-focus. They gave their son the contact information of a good counselor and the addiction recovery program at their church, and an ultimatum to get help or live somewhere else. They stood their ground and avoided wiping out in their relationship with God and each other. With time, and enough pain, their son decided to get the help he needed, but he still refused to turn to God and fully repent. Consequently, he will continue to suffer until he and his wife reconcile with God first and then with each other. When there is a need to reconcile with grown children, parents, siblings, or others, this can create stress in a marriage. It takes prayer and supernatural strength to stand together and stay focused on God to avoid getting in God's way while watching others we love suffer.

For You to Consider:

Is there anyone that you or your spouse needs to reconcile with? Are you facing tribulations in your marriage as a result of someone else's behavior and refusal to live a godly life? The Lord wants to help you reconcile with Him and with others. If you've prayed to Him and you feel He hasn't answered, you may have forgotten His promises. He always answers and He will never leave you nor forsake you (see Hebrews 13:5).

Action:

Read 1 Thessalonians 5:15-24, and answer the following questions.

1. What should you not do when someone wrongs you?

2. What should you continually do?

3. What should you hold on to? What should you avoid?

4. How is the "One who calls us" described?

Read Matthew 5:44-48, Romans 12:21, and 1 Corinthians 4:12- 13a.

If possible, try to go to dinner, dessert, or coffee with your spouse this week. Spend time with one another, and review what you have learned in class or in your group over the last few weeks. Don't put pressure on one another, but if possible, discuss how you might begin praying together daily. Also discuss how you can pray for one another on a regular basis.

> Prayer is the key to avoiding a wipe-out with God and each
> other. If you pray with and for each other daily, you will
> create supernatural protection for your marriage.

Please answer Discussion Questions on the next page.

LESSON FIVE DISCUSSION QUESTIONS

Please remember to be sensitive and respectful toward your spouse when sharing anything about your marriage relationship.

1. Can you think of a time that you suffered "a little while" before God restored you?

2. Have you and your spouse shared in a suffering together that you feel you could share with your group?

3. Which area is the most difficult for you concerning what to do when someone wrongs you? Why would this be so important in a marriage relationship?

4. What does this lesson say is the key to not wiping out?

5. Why would this be important to do for and with your spouse? Do you pray with your spouse?

Close in Prayer

LESSON SIX
KICKIN' OUT

After you ride a wave of tribulation in your marriage (or any other area of your life), will you relax and kick back, or will you stay on your suffer-board and kick out to catch the next wave?

"We hear that some among you are idle. They are not busy; they are busybodies. Such people we command and urge in the Lord Jesus Christ to settle down and earn the bread they eat. And as for you, brothers, never tire of doing what is right" (2 Thessalonians 3:11-13).

There are times when a surfer will choose to use the power of a wave's own force to kick his surfboard around while he's still on top of the wave in order to catch another wave. In surfing terms, this is referred to as kickin' out. After suffering through a tribulation in life, there will be times when all you'll want to do is relax. But we need to be careful that we don't get so comfortable that we miss an opportunity to use our experience to help others. It was never our Lord's intention that we quietly rest forever after we receive His supernatural power. The tribulations in life were not meant to wear you out; they were meant to strengthen you. The more waves you ride with your spouse, the stronger your marriage will be.

"The meaning of trial is not only to test our worthiness, but to increase it; as the oak is not only tested by the storms, but toughened by them." — Mrs. Charles E. Cowman, Streams in the Desert.

When we refer to kickin' out (as opposed to riding a wave of tribulation), there's a difference. In riding a wave of tribulation, the wave (trouble) just comes and you have no choice. But you can choose to either surf (suffer) your way and wipe out or choose God's way on your suffer-board and ride on top of the wave. In kickin out, you choose to use the wave you are now riding to help catapult you back in the direction of another wave for the purpose of sharing God's supernatural power with others. Kickin' out will allow your tribulation wave to become a living testimony for other "surfers" (sufferers), thus helping them learn to ride their suffer-boards during their own tribulations.

From Joe and Michelle Williams:

"A year or so after we reconciled, we felt a strong desire to help in the area of troubled marriages. We knew from our own experience that the church was not very well equipped in the area of helping those who were separated, and we knew that God wanted us to give back the same comfort to others that He had shown us. We started helping by serving in a small class at our church, and then wrote a workbook that became international (Reconciling God's Way, and revised ten years later as Marriage 911: First Response). Eventually we wrote a book, Yes, Your Marriage Can Be Saved, and it was published by Focus on the Family/Tyndale House—not because we were biblical scholars or well-known psychologists—but because our own marriage was saved and the publisher believed we could help others from that perspective. In the workbook and book, we share all of the important principles and tools that we learned to save our own marriage and help others save theirs."

Action:

1. Look up 2 Corinthians 1:3-4, and answer the following questions. What does God do when we have troubles?

2. What are we expected to do after our trouble?

3. What wave of tribulation have you experienced in your marriage (or other area in your life) when the Lord comforted you? Have you been able to comfort someone else in that area yet?

From Michelle:

"I was very close to my father when he passed away from cancer. Before he died, I used to send sympathy cards to people who had lost a parent, but it was only after I received sympathy cards that I fully understood what it felt like to be on the other end. Now, when I send a card to someone, I'm able to say things that I couldn't before, because I really understand their pain."

From Joe:

"Too many people sit in the pews (pronounced 'p-ewes' when used in this context) stinkin' because they never serve anywhere. Many of them have come through storms and tribulations in their lives—especially in the area of marriage—and their experiences could help so many others. The Lord didn't fill us with His living water to just let it sit and become stagnant. It's meant to flow through us to others."

For You to Consider:

Just as a surfer needs to be physically fit to kick out and catch another wave, you will need to be fit also. If you are physically, emotionally, and spiritually drained when you reach shore, you will not have the momentum to kick out and help others. Even Jesus and His disciples rested. But one thing to remember when resting between waves—especially before choosing to kick out—is to rest in prayer and time with God. This is not idle resting; it is active, through prayer and spending time in God's Word that you will grow stronger between waves and eventually be able to kick out to help others.

From Joe and Michelle:

"When we first began serving in ministry, we found that we weren't able to 'kick out' very often. We would make the mistake of trying to help others learn to ride their waves before we were rested and prayed-up from riding our own. But after much practice, we learned to pace ourselves and do what was necessary for our own personal and family temperament styles in order to be fit in all areas of our life. Several years ago, we went through a tribulation (we refer to it as our 'tsunami') with one of our children. Because we had learned to 'kick out' on a regular basis, we were able to help our grown child ride the wave while we maintained our ministry obligations. However, we did choose to say no to adding new speaking opportunities during that time, and we spent considerably more time getting spiritually and emotionally prepared before we added any new projects in our life. We also learned the importance of relying on others and delegating in ways we hadn't done before."

For You to Consider:

If you have never been able to ride a wave of tribulation and have enough energy left to kick out, continue practicing with your suffer-board, and God will lift you with His supernatural power to do so.

Action:

1. Look up Philippians 4:12-13. What does this verse promise regardless of the wave you are riding? Where does the strength come from?

2. In 1 John 3:18, what are we told to avoid doing?

3. List ways you could accomplish this through your own experiences:

For You to Consider:

What has been the most difficult time in your life? What about in your marriage?

Action:

Which area have you experienced a wave of tribulation with your spouse or personally? {Check mark options}

_____ Marital problems

_____ Financial problems

_____ Health problems

_____ Legal problems

_____ Death or illness of a family member or loved one

_____ Caring for aging parents

_____ Parenting problems with young or grown children

_____ Relationship problems with family members

_____ Job-related problems

_____ Crime-related problems (such as victim of violence or a loved one being charged with a crime)

_____ Other

If possible, take time this week to discuss these areas with your spouse. There are ministry and community service opportunities in each area. Once you have come through your tribulation, pray about becoming equipped to kick out and help others.

Please answer Discussion Questions on the next page.

LESSON SIX DISCUSSION QUESTIONS

Please remember to be sensitive and respectful toward your spouse when sharing anything about your marriage relationship.

1. Have you and your spouse ever been able to help another couple because of a tribulation that you experienced in your own lives?

2. Has a couple been able to help you?

3. Share your comments and answers regarding any action items in this week's lesson.

4. What Scripture verses in this week's lesson helped you most?

5. Is there anything holding you back from wanting to help others either in a church or community setting?

Close in Prayer

LESSON SEVEN
SHOOTIN' THE CURL

Not all surfers (sufferers) have the control and strength to do what the world says looks impossible with their suffer-boards.

"For the message of the cross is foolishness to those who are perishing, but to us who are being saved it is the power of God. For it is written: 'I will destroy the wisdom of the wise; the intelligent I will frustrate '" (1 Corinthians 1:18-19).

When a surfer shoots the curl, bystanders make comments like, "That looks impossible—how do they do that!" or, "Not many people have that kind of focus!" Instead of riding a wave safely to shore, these surfers are shootin' the curl by taking the opportunity to surf through the center of the wave. Because of daily practice with their board, they're able to accomplish something a novice surfer wouldn't even try. When a person is living for Christ and allowing the Holy Spirit to accomplish miracles in their life, friends and family often make the same comments. Instead of riding their wave of tribulation safely to shore, they take advantage of an opportunity to go through the middle of their wave supernaturally. Because of experience and practice with their suffer-board, they're able to do things many Christians never even try. Shootin ' the curl in Christianity is more than just living a Christian life. It's choosing to be stretched beyond normal human nature and abilities in order to join God in what He is doing in the world, by drawing on His Super Nature and ability through the power of the Holy Spirit. All followers of Christ are called to join Him in this way, but few will respond.

"Supposing God tells you to do something which is an enormous test to your common sense, what are you going to do? At the bar of common sense Jesus Christ's statements may seem mad; but bring them to the bar of faith, and you begin to find with awestruck spirit that they are the words of God. We act like pagans in a crisis, only one out of a crowd is daring enough to bank his faith in the character of God." — Oswald Chambers, <u>My Utmost for His Highest</u>, May 30

You will always have an opportunity to kick out without a lot of practice, but shootin' the curl will require supernatural ability that only God will provide after you have passed the test of persevering under trial. This doesn't mean that once you fail a test, you will never be able to shoot the curl in your Christian walk. Remember when Jesus restored Peter after his fall? He not only got back on his suffer-board, but he did extraordinary things for Christ and His church through the tribulations he faced later. If the Lord has allowed suffering in your life as a Christian—either because of your choices or another's choices—He will always give you an opportunity to do more with your waves than just ride them to safety.

From Joe and Michelle:

"When we first began serving in this ministry, we never dreamed we would be asked to equip pastors and leaders in a reconciliation ministry. In the early 90's most churches didn't allow anyone with divorce in their pasts to be in any type of leadership. We felt that because we had divorce in our background (even though it was prior to our becoming Christians), and a two-year separation in our own marriage, that us being allowed to teach a Sunday school class in our church was a miracle in itself.

When God gave us His vision for a world-wide reconciliation ministry, we assumed that someone else would lead it because neither of us had a degree in theology or counseling. We prayed for several years for a pastor to come alongside with the same vision we had in order to take the ministry beyond the walls of our church. You can imagine our surprise when the workbook that we authored—simply to teach our Sunday morning class—became the vehicle to grow the ministry into an international organization. We may not have had formal education, but God used us with our own Ph.D. (Previous History in Divorce) to do something we thought would never happen. We will never get over the fact that God allowed us—'the man and woman at the well'—to bring hope to couples and individuals struggling to keep their marriages together. Because of the shame we felt from our past, we almost missed an opportunity to learn that with God all things are possible (see John 4:9-41 and Matthew 19:26)."

Don't let shame or pride become the reason for not stepping out in faith to serve the Lord. Be willing to allow Him to use your experiences—no matter how many times you have wiped out—in order to help others. So many Christians miss opportunities for the Lord to use them because they want to look "perfect" for others, or because they fear rejection. Both reasons are based on self-focus rather than God-focus. Shootin' the curl requires total concentration on God. You will have plenty of opportunities in life to practice on your suffer-board, but never more than in marriage. To have a marriage that glorifies God will require you to have the same concentration on your suffer-board that a surfer shootin' the curl must have on his surfboard. To show God's love to a spouse who has just hurt your feelings or made a choice that will cause you pain and suffering means that you will have to choose to ride through the "center of your wave" and get your focus off of yourself with God's supernatural strength.

For You to Consider:

Think back to a time in your marriage that you willingly gave up your "right to be right" in the middle of a tribulation. If you did it out of love for Christ, you will have felt a supernatural peace come over you and an unexpected emotion of love for your spouse. That's shootin' the curl. Chances are however, that most of the time that you have given up your "right to be right" you've done it unwillingly and not with the love of Christ as your motivation. That's riding a wave of tribulation, but that's not shootin' the curl. Do you see the difference? After you ride a wave of tribulation in your marriage, you won't always experience the peace and joy of the Lord even though you came through without wiping out. When you are shootin' the curl, you will always have God's peace and joy because it will be the Holy Spirit in you riding the wave. That is what will allow you to supernaturally forgive your spouse after an offense. Your "flesh" will demand your "rights" but the Spirit in you will desire to "shoot the curl."

Action:

Look up Galatians 5:16-23, and answer the following questions.

1. What is in conflict?

2. How is the sinful nature described?

3. List the fruits of the Spirit.

Please don't miss what we want to share with you in this lesson. By the world's standards, it seems nearly impossible for husbands and wives to forgive each other when wronged, reconcile after abuse or adultery, or treat each other with kindness when angry. But that is exactly what we are asked to do. It's not impossible with God's supernatural strength. If you want to experience marriage the way the Lord intended, you will have to practice and you will have to be willing to shoot the curl often. But the rewards are far greater than you can imagine.

From James:

"I didn't see it coming. One night when my wife was being quiet and distant, as she would do periodically, I asked if there was something wrong, expecting to hear the usual 'no, nothing'. Instead, she simply looked at me and said, 'Yes, I am in love with someone else and want a divorce.' My knees buckled and I felt like someone slugged me. I couldn't believe what I heard. We were high school sweethearts and we had two children. How could she be in love with someone else? The questions were flooding through my mind: when did she have time to fall in love with someone else? Who was it? How would we tell the kids? I was trying to speak but no words came. Finally, I began to weep. I was losing my wife to another man. How did it happen, and how could I save our marriage and family? We were both believers, and in that moment I begged God for help and direction. The next thing I knew I was telling her I forgave her. For the next several hours everything came out like a flood. All the questions and how our marriage had gotten to where it was ended up being an all-night discussion. We ended by making a mutual decision to spend the next year putting our marriage back together. As in most adulterous affairs, ours was not all my wife's fault. I had contributed to the breakdown too. Over the next year we put God first, boundaries in place when it came to having opposite-sex friends, and I made sure to spend weekends doing things with our family instead of vegetating in front of a television watching sports.

Our crisis happened a few years ago and we now help others whose marriages are in crisis. One of the questions I'm often asked is how I could so quickly forgive my wife that night. People want to know if I had to keep doing it. No, I didn't. The forgiveness I felt that night was not like anything I'd ever experienced. It was supernatural. It was so real and so deep, and it was the catalyst to my wife trusting me with everything she needed to tell me and that I needed to hear."

To model to your children, family, friends, and the world a Christ-centered marriage, rather than a crisis-centered marriage, will be more important than any words you will ever share about the gospel of Christ. Many Christians talk about Christ's love and forgiveness, but with such a high divorce rate within the church, words mean very little.

Action:

1. Look up Colossians 3:12-19 and list the virtues.

2. Ask a Christian friend of the same sex to hold you accountable for five weeks.

3. Choose one virtue each week from verse 12, and pray for the Lord to give you His supernatural power in order to express these traits to your spouse and children God's way. Ask your friend to pray for you for the five-week period. At the beginning of each week, tell them which virtue you are practicing and how well you did or didn't do the week before.

4. In verses 13-19, choose the weakness that you struggle with the most. (Just choose one for now) Do a word study on it by first looking up its definition in a dictionary. Then search the Scriptures to help you understand God's perspective on that particular area.

It is important that you allow the Spirit to control you—not your flesh—when doing this lesson. If you try to do this on your own, you will risk wiping out. But if you pray, stay on your suffer-board, and be accountable, you'll be doing this with God's power. Begin to pray now about how God will use the tribulations in your life to help others as you mature. With God's help and your willingness to please Him, you will begin to see a difference in your heart attitude—and that's where true change and Christian maturity take place.

After the five-weeks are over, you might want to continue meeting with your accountability partner. This is a great way to work on character traits throughout the year (review Romans 5:3).

Please answer Discussion Questions on the next page.

LESSON SEVEN DISCUSSION QUESTIONS

Please remember to be sensitive and respectful toward your spouse when sharing anything about your marriage relationship.

1. Have you ever experienced a "shootin' the curl" situation in your marriage? (Remember, this is not just riding a wave, it is choosing to obey God in the midst of suffering in a way that produces supernatural joy and behavior in the middle of a crisis.)

2. Have you and your spouse had an opportunity to experience this as a couple?

3. Discuss your responses to any For You to Consider questions in this week's lesson.

4. Discuss your responses to any of the action questions in this week's lesson.

5. If you have chosen a virtue from Colossians to work on for the next five weeks please share it with your group.

6. If you would like to, please share a weakness that you struggle with, and what you have found in Scripture to help you.

Close in Prayer

LESSON EIGHT
HANG TEN!

God's laws and His grace are both necessary to have a balanced Christ-centered life. Will you hang ten in your marriage or will you be off balance and hang it up?

"I am the Lord your God…You shall have no other gods before me" (Exodus 20:2-3).

When surfers "hang ten", all their toes hang over the edge of the front of their board, which is possible only if the surfer's body is in perfect balance. When a husband and wife have a Christ-centered marriage that honors and glorifies God, they have learned how to balance the tribulations in their marriage with God's love. Remember that God doesn't promise to get you out of unpleasant situations, but He will be with you to see you through them!

We like to say that God's ten-letter word for love is commitment, and that's what it will take to stay balanced, hang on to your suffer-board, and keep God first during the tough times. You can hang on to your board and hang ten, or you can stop focusing on God when times get tough and hang it up. You will never be able to control the waves that come or the choices your spouse will make in life, but you can control how you balance God's Word with your choices.

"Our Lord trusted no man; yet He was never suspicious, never bitter, never in despair about any man, because He put God first in trust; He trusted absolutely in what God's grace could do for any man." — Oswald Chambers. <u>My Utmost for His Highest</u>, May 31.

Regardless of the troubles you have in your marriage at this time, and whether or not your spouse has been willing to go through this workbook with you, you still have an obligation to the Lord to honor your marriage vows and obey His Word.

For You to Consider:

You only have total control over one person on earth—you. In marriage many spouses end up bickering about small things that have to do with behavior they have no control over. The sad thing is, that when a wave of tribulation hits, they have spent more time taking withdrawals out of their spouses emotional love tank, than they have deposited. As a result, each person is depleted and exhausted and there is little energy left for standing together as a couple against the wave. Regardless of what your spouse chooses to do, make a commitment to live life God's way. Deposit positive things into your spouse's emotional love tank, not expecting anything back in return. Will it be hard? Of course. Is it possible with God's help? Absolutely!

Action:

1. Make a list of your spouse's positive attributes. If you are having a difficult time thinking of some, it means that your spouse is not exhibiting them—at least to you. When was the last time you gave your spouse a meaningful compliment? Take time this week to tell your spouse something you appreciate about him or her. Then, tell someone else. Get into the habit of filling up your spouse's love tank. (For more about emotional love tanks, see resources from author Gary Chapman, such as Love Languages.)

2. Have you been able to make some positive changes in your life due to any of the lessons in this workbook? If not, what is keeping you from working on changing negative behavior in your life?

3. Have you been able to pray for your spouse (and others) when you feel that you are suffering because of their choices? If so, what have you experienced as a result?

4. Have you been able to help anyone less fortunate than yourself over the course of the class? If so, what has God shown you?

For You to Consider:

In learning to keep your life balanced in order to have a Christ-centered marriage, it will require that you take full responsibility for your Christian walk and your maturity in Christ. It is not your responsibility to make sure that your spouse does what's necessary to grow spiritually. It is your job, however, to make certain that you grow in order to be able to model Christ-like behavior if your spouse wipes out or makes a wrong choice that will affect your marriage relationship.

Action:

1. Look up Galatians 6:1-5.

2. There are several examples packed into these verses that explain balance in various areas of life. List as many as you can find.

3. Have you been able to go over any or all of your lessons with your spouse?

4. If you have attended or completed lessons with your spouse, what are some of the changes you've made in your marriage as a couple?

From Joe:

"Most of the men I talk with that are separated from their wives say that they realize now how out of balance their lives were prior to the separation. They provided and provided until they divided, and now they have no one to provide for! Their jobs and desires to 'keep up with the Jones' ended up causing exactly what they were trying to avoid."

From Michelle:

"Nearly all the women who attend the reconciliation classes have told me that if they had to choose between having a wonderful home and financial security or a man who followed the Lord and treated them with love, honor, and respect, they would choose the latter without a doubt. Many have said through tears that they would give it all up tomorrow for a man who loved God and made his decisions based on the Word rather than the world. I agree. When Joe came to the Lord and began loving me with the gentle love of Christ, everything else became secondary.

Action:

Look over the following list and mark any area that needs to be better balanced in your life. Place a 2 beside areas needing a lot of restructure and a 1 in areas needing some. (Use no mark in areas that are well balanced.)

_____ Quiet time with God/prayer (alone without spouse or group)

_____ Alone time with spouse (getting away overnight or date nights)

_____ Bible study (outside the home or having groups in)

_____ Ministry service or church activities (even serving God needs balancing!)

_____ Job outside home (working overtime or not working enough)

_____ Time with family (extended family as well as those at home)

_____ Personal hygiene (weight control, health, diet, etc.)

Total= _____

Scoring: If you have scored between 12 and 14, you need to do some serious restructuring. Your life is out of balance, and if a wave hits, you'll wipe out in a hurry! If you have scored between 8 and 11, you're doing pretty well but you should put a plan together to work on a couple of areas. If you scored between 2 and 7, congratulations! That is, unless your time with God and your spouse are not a 0 or 1. If your total points are only a 0 or 1, you have a bigger problem than balancing your time. You're hot-doggin' and you probably need to rethink your answers!

If possible, discuss your scores with your spouse and ask for advice as to how to better balance your time and activities as a family. Don't parent each other and don't try to be the Holy Spirit. Just look at this time as an opportunity to help one another be better balanced in the best interest of the whole family.

From Joe and Michelle:

"When we went into full-time ministry in 1999, we realized that we could do ministry seven days a week, eight hours a day if we allowed ourselves. There was always someone needing help, always a chapter to be written, always a class to teach, and always a Bible study to take. Even though we knew better than to not balance our time properly, we found ourselves so busy in the beginning that we were not spending as much time with our grown children and grandchildren. Finally, one of our children made a comment that caused us to realize we were out of balance. Our grown child whose own marriage was in crisis said, 'I feel like everyone else gets your best, and we get the left-overs.' Ouch. We did some serious evaluation of our time and it resulted in some major changes in our schedules and how we conducted the ministry. The funny thing is that we rearranged our priorities to include more family time with our kids and grandkids, and ended up getting more accomplished. Every now and then we have to revisit our schedules just to make sure we catch any area that is out of balance. Of course, our kids are happy to let us know too!"

For You to Consider:

Please review your answers from the previous lessons and look for any area that you have not yet been able to balance in your life. Self-control in these areas will help you have the balance you need in order to hang ten and ride any wave of tribulation that will come in your marriage or life. In order to ride the waves of tribulation and "hang ten" in your marriage, your priorities must be straight. Regardless of how well you are doing in the area of self-control, honesty, or balancing your life, if God is not first in your life and you don't spend time with your "suffer-board" daily, you will never be able to "hang ten" in your marriage. And eventually, when the waves of tribulation come, you will "wipe out."

IN CONCLUSION

The next time a wave comes, the prayer of this ministry team is that you will grab your "suffer-board" and eagerly ride your wave with the supernatural power of God keeping you on top. If you "wipe out," repent and jump back on. And if you find yourself "hot doggin'," get your focus off yourself and back on the "board."

"…in the world you will have tribulation; but be of good cheer, I have overcome the world" John 16:33 (NKJ).

Last Action:

Hang Ten: Make a copy of the Ten Commandments, and hang them somewhere that reminds you of God's love and His action plan for your life. Whatever situation you find yourself in when riding your waves in marriage or life, remember that God loves you and all the suffering you are going through will be used to grow you and help others. He cares more about your relationship with Him than He does about your marriage. Even if you don't feel Him, He's out there on the waves with you—you're never alone.

RIPPLES ON THE POND

A young boy made a toy boat and then went to sail it on a pond. While he was playing with it along the water's edge, the boat floated out beyond his reach. In his distress he asked an older boy to help him. Without saying a word, the older child picked up some stones and started to throw them toward the boat. The little boy became upset, for he thought that the one he had turned to for help was being mean. Soon, though, he noticed that instead of hitting the boat, each stone was directed beyond it, making a small ripple that moved the vessel a little nearer to the shore. Every throw of the stone was planned, and at last the treasured toy was brought back to his waiting hands.

Sometimes it seems as if God allows circumstances into our lives that are harming us and are without sense or plan. We may be sure, though, that these waves of trial are intended to bring us nearer to Himself, to encourage us to set our minds "on things above, not on earthly things" (Colossians 3:2). Because we are prone to drift away from Him, the Lord must discipline us to get us back on the right course (Hebrews 12:9- 11).
Author unknown.

Please answer Discussion Questions on the next page.

LESSON EIGHT DISCUSSION QUESTIONS

Please remember to be sensitive and respectful toward your spouse when sharing anything about your marriage relationship.

1. How did you score on your balance test? Did you make any personal changes as a result of your score?

2. Were you able to discuss this test with your spouse? If so, did you make any changes as a couple?

3. When you reviewed past lessons, what were the most meaningful for you?

4. What do you plan to do now that the course is over in terms of accountability and life changes?

5. Is there an area of ministry that you feel called to? How about a community service need?

Close in Prayer

GROUP DISCUSSION AND CLASS GUIDELINES

These guidelines are based on many years of conducting classes and small groups for couples. They aren't meant to constrain you in any way, but to help you avoid some of the mistakes our leaders have experienced in the past. Feel free to adjust accordingly, and contact the ministry with any suggestions or questions along the way.

1. Class Leaders

It's nice to have a couple lead this course together. They will open in prayer, share a little teaching, introduce testimony speakers, and release people to their discussion times. The leader's should be in good standing in the community and in their church, and have a marriage which is not in crisis (at least one year of not using the words 'divorce' or 'separation' when disagreeing, or other serious issues).

2. Class or Small Group

- If you are going to have a class with couples attending, we recommend that you have no more than 3 couples at a table plus the facilitator in order to give more time for sharing.
- If a couple would like to facilitate a discussion table, consider having only two other couples at the table.
- If you plan to reach out to couples whose marriages are presently in crisis, or who are separated, we strongly recommend that you have men only and women only tables, with facilitators being the same gender and not couple-led. This is especially helpful if these couples have just come through a Marriage 911 class, and are still vulnerable to a set-back. This also protects the leaders from burnout or getting in the middle of a couple's marital problems and feeling as if they must take sides.
- If you want to get creative and keep with the theme of the workbook, consider decorating the room with an ocean or Hawaiian theme for fun. (When we teach the class at our church we put up surfboards and have pineapples in the middle of the tables!)

3. Discussion Times

- Choose a facilitator that has a good relationship with people and with God.
- Keep the conversations on the discussion questions, and politely stop anyone who gets off track, explaining that the time allotted for discussion must be adhered to.
- When going through the discussion questions, always have the facilitator answer last and only if there is ample time. Let others share first.
- Ask those sharing to respect their spouse when answering the questions.

4. Testimonials

After the second week, it's fun to have testimonials to begin each class. Ask a couple from church or the community who have gone through a storm and come out with their marriage stronger, to come in and give a 20 or 30 minute testimony. (Avoid asking people in class who may still be going through a storm. They can always share next semester once their wave is over.)

5. Last Class

It's nice to have a pot-luck and invite any of the speakers from previous weeks to attend. A Hawaiian theme makes it easy to decorate. Since the last action exercise is "Hang Ten", many leaders have chosen to print the Ten Commandments on nice parchment paper and hand it out to the attendees and facilitators. When giving them out, they have included a Hawaiian lei and called each couple or person up to receive it at the end of class, prior to enjoying the pot-luck, and give a brief testimony as to how the class has helped them.

Please feel free to contact us with questions.

Marriage911Godsway.com

Email us: Info@Marriage911Godsway.com